Original title:
Echo of Self

Copyright © 2024 Swan Charm
All rights reserved.

Author: Kätriin Kaldaru
ISBN HARDBACK: 978-9908-1-2590-9
ISBN PAPERBACK: 978-9908-1-2591-6
ISBN EBOOK: 978-9908-1-2592-3

Songs Beneath the Surface

In the quiet depths they lie,
Whispers of dreams that drift and sigh.
Echoes muted, soft yet clear,
Songs of hope that draw us near.

Currents hide their gentle flow,
Beneath the waves, where secrets grow.
Melodies of a silent sphere,
Guiding hearts that long to hear.

With every pulse, the depths expand,
In unseen worlds, we take our stand.
Tales of life and love entwined,
Songs beneath that speak our mind.

Like the ocean's vast embrace,
We find our strength in hidden space.
Resonating deep within,
The silent tunes where we begin.

Listen close and you may find,
Harmony within the blind.
Songs beneath the waves will rise,
Carried forth, a sweet surprise.

The Pulse of Identity

In the heartbeat of our days,
A rhythm found in varied ways.
Threads of self in colors bold,
Weaving stories yet untold.

Shadows dance in sunlight's grace,
Every step, a different pace.
Navigating through the noise,
We define ourselves, our joys.

Moments flicker, quick like dreams,
Reflecting in our complex themes.
With each choice, a path reveals,
The pulse of self, it never heals.

Voices rise and intertwine,
In the chorus, we align.
Seeking truth among the lies,
The pulse of us beneath the skies.

In the silence, echoes ring,
All the songs of whom we sing.
Our identities, a vibrant throng,
Every heartbeat, pure and strong.

Distant Ripples of Thought

In the stillness, thoughts arise,
Casting ripples in the skies.
Waves of wonder, far and wide,
Echoes of the mind's deep tide.

Questions float on gentle streams,
Carried forth by fleeting dreams.
Each reflection, a story spun,
Distant ripples, never done.

Like a pebble tossed in time,
Ideas shimmer, soft, sublime.
In the vastness, thoughts take flight,
Distant ripples, pure delight.

A gentle breeze, a whispered thrill,
Stirring waves with passion's will.
What we ponder shapes our day,
Distant ripples guide our way.

As we linger, thoughts will grow,
In quiet moments, we'll bestow.
A tapestry of mind and heart,
Distant ripples, a work of art.

The Soul's Gentle Harmony

In the quiet of the night,
Soft notes weave their purest light.
Melodies that soothe the soul,
Gentle harmonies make us whole.

Every breath a tender sound,
In the silence, peace is found.
A symphony without a throng,
The soul's embrace, where we belong.

With each chord, a feeling wakes,
An echo of the love it takes.
Notes of joy and shades of blue,
The soul sings softly, sweet and true.

Like a river's steady flow,
Carving paths where we shall go.
In the music, we find grace,
The soul's gentle, sacred space.

So close your eyes and let it be,
The love within will set you free.
In harmony, we rise and sway,
The soul's sweet song, our guiding way.

The Light Within the Shadow

In the quiet hush of night,
Whispers flicker soft and bright.
Hidden truths in shadows play,
Guiding souls along their way.

Lost in realms of dark and light,
Searching for a spark so right.
In each corner, warmth does blend,
Showing hope that will not end.

Amidst the chaos, peace can grow,
Finding warmth in a heart's glow.
With every fear that fades from sight,
We embrace the coming light.

Unraveled Thoughts

In the silence, echoes roam,
Fragments searching for a home.
Whirling in a dizzy dance,
Thoughts collide, a fleeting chance.

Questions swirl in fervent flight,
Chasing shadows in the night.
Each idea, a thread unwound,
Lost in echoes, yet they're found.

Tangled in the webs we weave,
Moments pass, we hardly grieve.
Each reflection brings a sign,
Carving paths through tangled lines.

Woven Dreams

In the fabric of the night,
Lies a tapestry of light.
Stitched with hopes and silent fears,
Fragile as the morning tears.

Colors blend in hues divine,
Threads of fate, forever intertwine.
Every dream a whispered plea,
Woven softly, wild and free.

In the looms of restless minds,
Beauty blooms but often blinds.
Yet, in chaos, art is born,
From the dreams where we are torn.

Murmurs from a Distant Heart

From afar, a heartbeat calls,
Echoing through ancient halls.
Whispers of a love once known,
Lingering like a gentle tone.

Mistress of the moonlit sky,
Revealing secrets as they sigh.
Each murmur floats on midnight air,
Carrying wishes, sweet and rare.

In the stillness, longing grows,
As the heart's soft rhythm flows.
Though miles stretch between us wide,
Feel the pulse of love inside.

The Dance of Reflected Light

Beneath the waves, reflections twirl,
Creating stories in a swirl.
Each ripple, a dance, a song,
Carrying hopes where we belong.

In the sunlight's warm embrace,
We find dreams that interlace.
Dancing shadows in the breeze,
Whisper secrets through the trees.

As night unfolds its velvet cloak,
Life's mysteries softly spoke.
In the stillness, light takes flight,
Joining us in pure delight.

The Language of Solitude

In the hush of night, truths unfurl,
Whispers echo, a lone heart's swirl.
Stars above, silent and bright,
Guide the wanderer lost in light.

Shadows dance as dreams take flight,
Each breath a pulse, in soft twilight.
Alone but free, the soul finds peace,
In solitude's arms, sweet release.

Time suspends, moments blend,
In quietude, a faithful friend.
Each thought a leaf, drifting down,
In this stillness, I wear the crown.

The heart speaks loud in silent tones,
In every pause, love's essence roams.
Alone I stand, yet never bare,
In solitude, I find my prayer.

Embracing space, a sacred rite,
In solitude, I gain my sight.
Nature whispers, the breeze it sings,
In the heart's chamber, silence clings.

Memories Wrapped in Silence

In the corners of my mind, they dwell,
Soft echoes of stories, woven well.
Each glance a thread, each sigh a seam,
A tapestry of days, woven dreams.

Fading whispers of laughter's grace,
In shadows cast, I see their face.
Silent moments, bittersweet,
Wrapped in time, where past and present meet.

Pages turn in a book untold,
Fleeting glances, borrowed gold.
In solitude, these thoughts collide,
Memories wrapped in silence, where I confide.

The heart remembers, though time may fade,
In its own chamber, a gentle cascade.
Each heartbeat whispers secrets rare,
In silence echoing, memories declare.

And as the world spins in its dance,
I find myself in a wistful trance.
Memories linger, delicate threads,
In the loom of silence, love never dreads.

Gazing Into Depths of Thought

In stillness, I peer beyond the veil,
Waves of reflection, vast and pale.
Each thought a ripple, soft and slow,
In the depths of my mind, I delve below.

Questions swirl like autumn leaves,
In the quiet, the heart believes.
Gazing deep, I find the truth,
In the chambers where wisdom soothes.

The surface shimmers, a mirror clear,
Revealing shadows, what I fear.
In echoes deep, I hear my call,
In depths of thought, I rise, I fall.

With every glance, a world unfolds,
Stories waiting, secrets told.
In the silence, insight glows,
Gazing into the depth, the essence flows.

In quiet realms, my heart explores,
The boundaries of thought, infinite shores.
I dive beneath the surface bright,
In the depths of thought, I find the light.

The Timeless Arc of Self

In the mirror of time, I search my face,
Layers unravel, a haunting grace.
Each wrinkle a tale, each scar a sign,
In the arc of self, I redefine.

Moments linger, stitched in thread,
In the fabric of life, the paths I tread.
Every heartbeat sings its song,
In the timeless arc where I belong.

The past whispers soft in present's ear,
A dance of shadows, a waltz sincere.
Each choice a stepping stone, each laugh a bell,
In this journey of self, I know me well.

Fading echoes of who I used to be,
Resonate softly, a memory.
In the stories told, my truth emerges,
The timeless arc of self, it converges.

Through storms and calm, I find the way,
In the journey of self, I choose to stay.
Embracing all, I stand as one,
In the cycle of life, my threads are spun.

The Chorus of My Thoughts

In quiet rooms, whispers bloom,
A symphony in the dim light.
Words like shadows start to loom,
Dancing softly, taking flight.

Echoes ring through time and space,
Each note a fragment of the day.
Haunting melodies we embrace,
In the silence, they will stay.

With every breath, the chorus grows,
Stories woven into sound.
In the heart, the heartbeat flows,
A hidden world that knows no bounds.

Through the chaos, there's a song,
Resonating deep within.
A reminder that we belong,
In the rhythm, we begin.

So let the voices softly play,
A harmony of dreams untold.
In the night that turns to day,
The chorus wraps us in its fold.

Flickers of Inner Light

In shadows cast by doubts and fears,
A spark ignites, a glow begins.
It dances through the pain and tears,
An ember where the hope now spins.

A flicker bright in darkest hours,
A quiet flame that won't go out.
It threads through life like blooming flowers,
Defying all the weight of doubt.

When storms arise and skies turn gray,
This light will guide the weary feet.
A beacon through the disarray,
In every moment, bittersweet.

Hold tight to those small sparks of grace,
Each flicker whispers to the soul.
With every breath, we find our place,
In the warmth, we all feel whole.

Let inner light show you the way,
Through the night, it starts to gleam.
In chaos, let your heart sway,
Toward the truth that lights your dream.

The Diary of a Dreamer

Pages filled with whispered dreams,
Ink that flows like rivers wide.
In moonlit nights, imagination gleams,
A world where hopes and fears collide.

Sketches of places yet unseen,
Each line a pathway to explore.
With every thought, a vibrant scene,
In the quiet, yearning for more.

Dreams take flight on wings of light,
A canvas painted with desire.
Every word, a soaring kite,
Lifting higher, dreams aspire.

From dawn to dusk, the stories flow,
Captured in this gentle space.
Adventures through the undertow,
In the diary, we embrace.

Let dreams unfold like petal's grace,
With courage woven into lines.
In the heart, we find our place,
A dreamer's world where magic shines.

Threads of Forgotten Voices

Whispers lost in time's embrace,
Threads of stories intertwine.
Voices echo, leave their trace,
Carrying secrets divine.

In the silence, wisdom stirs,
A tapestry of life unfolds.
Each thread, a song that gently purrs,
Weaving memories like gold.

Forgotten tales now dance in dreams,
Fading echoes call us near.
In shadows, they form vibrant beams,
Reminding us that hope is clear.

Listen closely to the sound,
Of forgotten hearts that still beat.
In the silence, truth is found,
A connection so bittersweet.

May we honor every voice,
In the stories yet to come.
Embrace the past, make our choice,
To carry forth what we become.

Embraces of Muted Whispers

In twilight's hush, a soft caress,
Voices linger, secrets confess.
Amongst the shadows, dreams unfold,
The heart's language, tenderly told.

Flickering flames in the stillness dance,
Echoes of memories, lost in a glance.
Every heartbeat, a gentle sigh,
Wrapped in silence, the night draws nigh.

Softly we breathe, in the quiet air,
Finding solace in the moments we share.
Whispers weave through our tangled minds,
In the stillness, peace gently finds.

Under the stars, our spirits align,
In the embrace of whispers, we intertwine.
Timeless secrets in the dark arise,
Filling the void beneath endless skies.

Through the murmurs, a love that glows,
In muted whispers, true essence flows.
Together we'll linger, as shadows play,
Eternal dancers in the fading day.

The Soliloquy of Time

Time weaves stories in a silent thread,
Each passing moment, a word unsaid.
The hands of the clock in rhythm sway,
Pulling us gently, then fading away.

In the shadows of dusk, we reminisce,
Fleeting moments like whispers of bliss.
The past and future in delicate lace,
Eternally bound in a warm embrace.

Memories echo in the silence vast,
Fleeting memories from a long-lost past.
The ticking clock speaks in a gentle hum,
Marking the steps of the days yet to come.

With every heartbeat, the present flows,
In time's embrace, certainty grows.
Dancing gently on this fragile line,
In the soliloquy, we find what's divine.

As dawn breaks bright, new tales unfold,
In golden sunlight, dreams to behold.
Time whispers softly, a constant refrain,
A timeless journey through joy and pain.

Reflections on a Still Pond

Glistening waters kiss the pine,
Mirrored worlds in a dance divine.
Ripples of thought, a gentle press,
Nature reveals her silent finesse.

Clouds etch stories on the blue,
Carried by breezes, whispers anew.
The sun bows low, in reverent awe,
As shadows lengthen, revealing a flaw.

Wandering eyes trace the horizon wide,
In stillness, the soul is a tranquil tide.
Gentle reflections of what should be,
An echo of dreams that yearn to be free.

Awash in colors from dusk till dawn,
Each moment captured, never withdrawn.
Life's fleeting essence floats on the glass,
In the pond's embrace, we watch time pass.

Amongst the lilies, secrets lie still,
Whispering softly the echoes of will.
Within each ripple, a tale to spin,
Reflections of life, where dreams begin.

Imprints of the Untraveled Road

Beneath the canopy of whispering trees,
The untraveled road beckons with ease.
Footprints carved in the earth's embrace,
Every journey begins with a trace.

With every bend, the unknown calls,
Ancient echoes between the walls.
Stories linger in the air so thick,
Imprints of choices, each step we pick.

Winding pathways through fields of gold,
Unfolding stories yet to be told.
The heart races in a rhythmic dance,
In solitude's comfort, we take a chance.

Stars above guide the wandering soul,
With lanterns of hope, making us whole.
Through dusk's embrace, the adventure grows,
In every shadow, the light still glows.

As horizons stretch, our spirits soar,
With dreams unbound, we crave for more.
On the untraveled road, we find our way,
In the imprints left, we choose to stay.

Reflections in a Still Pool

In the calm water, the sky bends,
Clouds float gently, time suspends.
Leaves whisper secrets, a soft call,
Echoes of nature, binding us all.

Ripples dance, a fleeting trace,
Mirrors of thoughts in a sacred space.
Each moment captured, clear and bright,
In stillness, dreams take flight.

The swaying reeds, they softly sway,
Telling tales of a golden day.
Sunlight glimmers, a warm embrace,
In this still pool, we find our place.

Reflections shimmer, truths unfold,
Stories of the heart, quietly told.
Beneath the surface, depths unknown,
In tranquil waters, wisdom is sown.

With every ripple, a choice is made,
In the stillness, our fears do fade.
In the quiet, we listen and learn,
For the soul's reflections, we yearn.

Whispers of the Inner Voice

In the silence, a voice calls clear,
Soft and gentle, for hearts that hear.
Guiding us through the darkest night,
A whisper of truth, a beacon of light.

Thoughts unravel like threads of gold,
Stories of courage, waiting to be told.
In every heartbeat, a promise lies,
To trust our journey, to rise and fly.

When shadows gather and doubt descends,
The inner voice speaks, a loyal friend.
It tells of strength, of paths unfound,
In tranquil moments, our hopes abound.

Listen closely, let silence reign,
In whispered secrets, we break the chain.
For in our hearts, the answer stays,
Guiding us gently through maze-like days.

Embrace the visions, let them be known,
For whispers of the soul, they make us whole.
In the quiet, the universe sings,
Trust the whispers, the hope it brings.

Reverberations of the Soul

In the depths of night, echoes sing,
Resonating softly, a sacred ring.
Chords of presence, heavy and light,
Reverberating through the endless night.

A melody weaves in tender threads,
Connecting the heart, where silence spreads.
Each note a whisper, both near and far,
Guiding our path, like a fading star.

From valleys low to mountains high,
The song of the soul will never die.
It dances in shadows, it glows in light,
A symphony crafted, a glorious sight.

Feel the vibrations, let them swell,
In the language of spirit, we dwell.
The pulse of existence, a timeless rhyme,
Reverberating through the fabric of time.

And as we listen, the world aligns,
In harmony bound, our heart entwines.
For every echo carries a dream,
A silent assurance, a gentle beam.

Shadows of My Being

In the quiet dusk, shadows creep,
Echoing memories, secrets they keep.
Fleeting figures dance with grace,
In twilight's embrace, we find our place.

The past lingers softly, a tender shade,
Whispering lessons in light and fade.
Each shadow a story, a fragment of time,
In their depths, we find reason and rhyme.

Winds of change sweep through the night,
Carving paths filled with whispers of light.
The shadows reflect what we try to hide,
In their presence, the truth won't subside.

I walk with the echoes of all I've known,
In the shadows, the seeds I've sown.
They shape my being, they guide my way,
In the dance of darkness, I learn to stay.

With each step forward, the shadows wane,
Bringing forth strength from all the pain.
In the interplay of light and gloom,
The shadows of my being find room.

Notes from an Untouched Place

In a forest deep, I wander slow,
Whispers of leaves in a soft, sweet flow.
Sunlight dances on emerald hue,
Nature's secrets, so pure and true.

A brook flows gently, a timeless song,
Each pebble glimmers, where dreams belong.
Here, the air is rich with grace,
In every corner, life finds its place.

Birds sing sweetly, a choir above,
Carving the silence, a hymn of love.
Clouds drift lazily, shadows embrace,
In this untouched realm, I find my space.

Time stands still, as moments blend,
An endless journey with no end.
With every breath, I feel the peace,
In this sanctuary, my heart's release.

A place untouched, where spirits rise,
Under the vast, unclouded skies.
I gather notes from the gentle breeze,
In this untouched place, my soul finds ease.

The Tapestry of Inner Voices

In the stillness of night, I hear a call,
A whispering thread, weaving through all.
Voices of dreams, both near and far,
Painting my thoughts like constellations' spar.

Each thread a story, a truth, a plea,
Unraveling softly, setting me free.
Layers of silence, of joy and dread,
In this tapestry, my heart is led.

The voices murmur, like rivers they flow,
Carving through shadows, they gently bestow.
Lessons of life, both bitter and sweet,
In the fabric of being, our destinies meet.

I listen closely, to echoes of old,
Of courage, of fear, of tales untold.
Woven together, the brave and the meek,
In this inner realm, I find what I seek.

A myriad whispers, a symphonic dance,
In the quiet of night, I take my chance.
Embracing the chorus, I rise and rejoice,
In the tapestry woven, I hear my true voice.

Lost Melodies of the Soul

In the silence, echoes play their tune,
Haunting the twilight beneath the moon.
Melodies hidden, in shadows conceal,
Unfinished symphonies they gently reveal.

Notes of longing drift through the air,
Whispers of heartstrings, a fragile flare.
Each chord a memory, sweet yet bittersweet,
In the quiet, the past and present meet.

Fleeting harmonies called back in time,
Rhythms of laughter, in a soft chime.
Ghosts of melodies dance on the breeze,
Carried on winds, providing a tease.

A song forgotten, yet deep within,
Stirs the essence, where hope begins.
Fragments of music, like stars they align,
In the lost melodies, my heart starts to shine.

I gather these whispers, the notes of yore,
Trusting their journey to guide me once more.
In the tapestry woven, my spirit will soar,
Finding the rhythm that I long to explore.

The Stillness of Unseen Currents

Beneath the surface, where shadows play,
Unseen currents guide the day.
A pulse of silence, strong and deep,
In the stillness, secrets sleep.

Waves of tranquility, a gentle embrace,
Softly cradling the human race.
In this stillness, wisdom flows,
And in its depths, the heart knows.

Ripples of thought dance in the mind,
Where clarity rests and peace is kind.
In the quiet, the soul can breathe,
In these unseen currents, hope weaves.

A reflection of dreams, of skies above,
Carried by currents of universal love.
In the calm, my spirit glides,
As stillness shelters, where truth abides.

Here, time unravels in gentle waves,
In unseen currents, the heart behaves.
A journey inward, serene and bright,
In this hushed realm, I find my light.

Veils of Introspection

Behind the mirror, shadows play,
Thoughts entwined in soft decay.
Whispers lost in grains of time,
Searching for a silent rhyme.

Faded echoes softly call,
Tugging at the mind's old hall.
Layers cloak the heart's bright light,
Veils of deep within the night.

Curious glances search the soul,
Pieces longing to be whole.
In the stillness, truth takes form,
Quiet storms begin to warm.

Fragments dance in twilight's glow,
Every thought a hidden show.
Delicate, the threads unwind,
Veils reveal what's left behind.

Nights of pondering pass me by,
Underneath a watchful sky.
Awakening in silence rare,
Finding solace in the air.

The Art of Being Unheard

In corners dark, a voice won't rise,
Silent truths behind the guise.
Words are lost, like whispers thin,
While noise surrounds, they fade within.

Every heartbeat tells a tale,
Of dreams that shiver, softly pale.
Yet, in shadows thoughts take flight,
Crafting art in muted sight.

A canvas blank, emotions pour,
Ink of silence, yearning for more.
In stillness lies a vibrant hue,
Painting worlds both old and new.

Elegance in the unsaid grace,
Finding strength in a quiet space.
Invisible threads weave through the air,
Creating bonds that few may share.

Listening closely, hearts might find,
In whispered secrets, peace of mind.
The boldest stories never told,
In the hush, the world unfolds.

Echoes linger, softly blent,
In the silence, voices spent.
Yet there's power, deeply stirred,
In the art of being unheard.

Cadence of the Unsung

In the silence, rhythms bound,
Where the lost and lonely sound.
Songs of heart that no one hears,
Whispers trailing through the years.

Each note lingers on the breeze,
Carried softly through the trees.
Echoes of a life once bright,
Cadence dances in the night.

Unseen artists paint the sky,
With stardust dreams that float on high.
Hands that brush away the gray,
Creating light in shades of play.

Rhythms hidden, secrets hum,
In the stillness, life can come.
Layers deep with stories spun,
A symphony of the unsung.

In every street, a tale concealed,
Hope revived, a fate revealed.
Every heart, a song to share,
In quiet moments, kindness rare.

Listen close, the world will sing,
To the pulse that love can bring.
Open ears and open hearts,
Discover where the magic starts.

Fables Whispered in the Dark

Underneath a velvet sky,
Tales of wonder weave and fly.
Fables whispered, shadows creep,
Secrets cradle within sleep.

Ancient stories softly swirl,
Lost in time, their voices twirl.
Myths and legends, dimmed yet bright,
Flicker like the stars at night.

With every sigh, a tale begins,
Of timeless lands, of losses, wins.
In the dusk, the moments spark,
Fables whispered in the dark.

Embers flicker, hearts ignite,
Latch on to the fragile light.
Through the whispering shadows tread,
Find the words that once were said.

In the quiet, magic brews,
An unseen path, a world of hues.
Among the dreams, a truth will hark,
Fables whispered in the dark.

The Resonance Within

In silence deep, I hear the call,
A whisper soft that breaks through all.
Echoes dance in chambers wide,
For in my heart, the truth will guide.

The beating drum, a steady sound,
Resonates where dreams abound.
In shadows cast, I find the light,
Awakening the spark in night.

Each thought a wave, each breath a breeze,
Woven through the ancient trees.
The pulse of life, a rhythmic tune,
Bringing forth the fading moon.

With every note, a story spun,
Of battles lost and victories won.
In harmony, I find my place,
In the chorus of time and space.

So let the music swell and rise,
With every beat, the spirit flies.
For in this dance, I am alive,
In resonance, I truly thrive.

Conversations with the Mirror

I stand before this fragile glass,
A silent friend, the moments pass.
With every glance, a question posed,
What lies within, what is enclosed?

Reflections show more than the skin,
Deep within, where thoughts begin.
Each wrinkle tells a tale untold,
Of dreams once bright, now faint and cold.

I see the years painted on my face,
Wisdom blooms, yet leaves a trace.
In quietude, we share our fears,
The mirror captures all my tears.

As shadows dance and visions fade,
The truth I seek is not delayed.
In whispers soft, the answers flow,
In this stillness, I learn to grow.

So here I stand, no need to hide,
Embracing all that's left inside.
For in this glass, I find my peace,
A dialogue that will not cease.

Fragments of My Soul

Scattered pieces, old and new,
Each fragment tells a tale, it's true.
In shadows thick where silence dwells,
The stories linger, cast their spells.

A laugh once joyful, a tear once shed,
Memories dance where angels tread.
In whispers soft, the past unfolds,
A tapestry of dreams and golds.

The heart remembers every song,
In every right, there's often wrong.
These fragments weave a life well lived,
Through trials faced and love received.

So gather close, these bits of light,
Each shining shard, a star in night.
Together they create my whole,
A masterpiece, the art of soul.

In every piece, a lesson stays,
One life crafted in many ways.
Embracing all that I've become,
In fragments found, my heart is home.

Songs of the Unseen Heart

Within the quiet, soft and still,
A melody begins to thrill.
The unseen heart, a hidden song,
In the shadows where we belong.

Each note a memory, sweet and rare,
Whispered secrets fill the air.
In rhythm pulse, the night awakes,
As silence breaks, the spirit shakes.

Harmonies from depths untold,
A symphony of brave and bold.
In every beat, a story flows,
Of dreams and fears, of love that grows.

So let the music fill the skies,
A chorus sung where freedom lies.
Each unseen heart, a songbird's call,
Together in this space, we fall.

In waves of sound, we find our way,
A tapestry of night and day.
For in the song, we find our worth,
The unseen heart, our place on Earth.

Notes from an Inner Sanctuary

In silence I find solace,
Soft echoes of my heart,
Whispers of the past remain,
Guiding light, a brand new start.

Each thought like fragile petals,
Floating on a gentle stream,
Fragrant hopes, they dance and swirl,
Entwined within a dream.

Through shadows of contemplation,
I uncover hidden sights,
Mountains carved by ancient tears,
Together we ignite the nights.

A sanctuary built with care,
Walls adorned with tales untold,
The warmth of inner laughter,
A refuge to behold.

With each note a story whispers,
Melodies of joy and pain,
In this place I weave my freedom,
Where barriers break like chains.

Reflections in the Abyss

Deep down where shadows linger,
A mirror shows my soul's plight,
Waves crash with endless fervor,
In the depths, I seek the light.

Fragments of a fractured past,
Sinking thoughts, like ships at sea,
Caught within the swirling tides,
I search for peace, to be free.

Whispers of forgotten sorrows,
Echo through the midnight air,
Haunting dreams that linger still,
On this journey, I must dare.

The abyss holds shards of wisdom,
In shadows, truth is revealed,
Lessons learned through anguished cries,
A path to hope, unconcealed.

With courage as my compass,
I'll navigate these darkened ways,
For even in the deepest void,
A flicker of hope can blaze.

Whispers of the Inner Tide

In the quiet of the evening,
Waves of thought begin to rise,
Carrying secrets softly,
Beneath the vast, starry skies.

Each current flows with meaning,
Guiding me through reverie,
Where the heart and mind converge,
In tranquil harmony.

A tide shaped by fleeting moments,
Rippling patterns on the shore,
Echoes of a gentle laughter,
Calling me to dream once more.

Through the whispers of the water,
I am swept into the night,
Trusting in the inner pull,
Finding solace in the light.

In this dance of ebb and flow,
I embrace the shifting sands,
For within the inner tide,
I discover where my heart stands.

Shadows of Forgotten Dreams

In the corners of my memory,
Shadows roam and softly sigh,
Faded dreams, they echo gently,
In the night, they linger nigh.

Once vibrant hues now muted,
Rustling like the autumn leaves,
In their twilight, they remind me,
Of the hopes that time deceives.

Forgotten paths, once brightly lit,
Now obscured by doubts and fears,
Yet, in these shadows lies a spark,
A reminder of past years.

Each dream, a story waiting,
For the courage to arise,
To bring them back to daylight,
Beneath the vast and open skies.

In the shadows, I find beauty,
In the quiet, strength can grow,
For within the depths of dreaming,
Resilience starts to show.

Subtle Currents of Existence

In whispers soft, the shadows play,
A dance of thoughts that fade away,
Time drifts like leaves on rivers wide,
Embracing all that flows inside.

The heartbeats pulse in silent space,
Each moment carries a tender trace,
A symphony of quiet dreams,
Where nothing's ever as it seems.

The stars above, they weave the tales,
Of endless journeys, ancient sails,
In the stillness, truth reveals,
The depth of life that time conceals.

With every breath, a new design,
In fleeting hues, our lives entwine,
The currents pull, both fierce and light,
Guiding us through the tranquil night.

Amidst the chaos, stillness found,
In every whisper, a sacred sound,
We drift along these subtle streams,
Awakening to hidden dreams.

Portraits in Silent Hues

Brushstrokes mingle, colors blend,
In quiet corners, stories bend,
Each canvas holds a soul's retreat,
Where silence wraps the heart's heartbeat.

The shadows linger, softly drawn,
Emotions painted with the dawn,
Eyes that tell what words cannot,
In shades of love and battles fought.

Whispers echo, the colors sigh,
In twilight's grasp, the spirits fly,
Each portrait breathes a sacred song,
In the gallery where dreams belong.

With gentle hands, the artist weaves,
The laughter caught among the leaves,
In silent hues, the world awakes,
As memory through the canvas breaks.

A tapestry of time unfolds,
In every hue, a truth retold,
The portraits gaze, forever still,
Within their frames, they bend our will.

Waves of the Forgotten Self

Beneath the surface, echoes hide,
Remnants of the soul's long ride,
Waves crash softly on the shore,
   Carrying tales of evermore.

In the depths, where shadows play,
Old dreams drift gently, night to day,
Yearning whispers call us home,
Where the heart learns once again to roam.

Tides that pull, then push away,
In the silence, we find our way,
Forgotten selves in fleeting light,
Rising from the depths of night.

With every ripple, life resumes,
Through watery paths, the spirit blooms,
Awakening in sapphire hues,
Lost and found in ocean's muse.

In every crest, a story flows,
In every trough, a truth that glows,
Waves that crash and softly swell,
   Mark the journey of the self.

Songs Sung to the Night

In velvet dusk, the stars ignite,
Melodies weave into the night,
Whispers of dreams in moonlight fair,
Sweet serenades fill the air.

The crickets play their ancient tune,
Beneath the watchful silver moon,
Each note a wish, a hopeful sigh,
Carried on the breeze, they fly.

The darkness hums with tales untold,
In shadows, secrets unfold,
Songs that stir the sleeping heart,
In every end, a new start.

With gentle hands, the night composes,
A symphony of fragrant roses,
In every silence, songs appear,
Echoing love, dispelling fear.

As dawn approaches, songs may fade,
Yet in our hearts, their echoes laid,
For every night, a story spun,
Forever sung, till day is done.

The Symphony of Inner Echoes

In the chamber where silence dwells,
Soft whispers rise like gentle spells.
Each note, a peak of fleeting grace,
Resonates within this sacred space.

Chords of memory, faint yet clear,
Speak of joy, and trace of fear.
Harmony of shadows in my mind,
A melody of truths entwined.

Like ripples dancing on a stream,
Each thought, a fragment of a dream.
Notes of laughter, cries entwined,
An echo of what I left behind.

Through the rhythm, I find my way,
Steps of light and shades of gray.
The symphony plays, timeless and bold,
In the heart's recess, stories unfold.

As the final note begins to fade,
I embrace the music that I've made.
For in this symphony of mine,
Lie the echoes of a life divine.

Threads of My Own Canvas

With colors bright, I weave my tale,
In gentle strokes, where dreams set sail.
A tapestry of hopes and fears,
Each thread holds laughter, marks of tears.

The shades of blue, reflect my soul,
In every hue, I find my role.
Emerald whispers, burnt sienna sighs,
Capture the moments that soar and rise.

Each section tells a story true,
Of love held fast and friendships new.
Crimson marks the passion's spark,
Stitching the light into the dark.

As I create my sacred space,
In every line, I find my grace.
Threads entwined, in harmony dance,
A work of art, born from my chance.

In the gallery of my own heart,
Each canvas crafted, a work of art.
With every stroke, I come alive,
In the threads of life, I learn to thrive.

The Breath of Unspoken Fears

In shadowed corners of my mind,
Lurks a presence, undefined.
Whispers swirl in the quiet night,
A breath held tight, out of sight.

Fear of failure, fear of loss,
Crossing rivers that seem like dross.
Yet within the stillness, I find peace,
In the silence, doubts may cease.

Each heartbeat echoes, soft and slow,
Through the struggle, I learn to grow.
Fears like clouds may block the sun,
But in their shroud, I am still one.

Breath by breath, I face the storm,
Embracing all, in every form.
The unspoken fears may always be,
Yet they guide me towards the free.

In acceptance, I take my stand,
Holding the fate of my own hand.
With courage born from whispers near,
I rise anew, beyond all fear.

Portraits of Wandering Feelings

In colors soft, emotions blend,
Brush strokes of love, where hearts transcend.
Each portrait holds a truth untold,
Of fleeting moments, brave and bold.

A gaze that lingers, shadows cast,
Captures echoes of the past.
Every hue, a feeling known,
On canvas deep, my heart has grown.

From joy's bright laughter, to sorrow's sighs,
In every masterpiece, a glimpse of skies.
Wandering feelings, timeless and free,
Painted whispers of what can be.

Through every layer, I explore,
The palette of life, I can't ignore.
In each detail, the stories flow,
Portraits showing love's soft glow.

As I wander through this artful maze,
Each brush of thought, a silent praise.
In portraits framed by tears and smiles,
I find my truth across these miles.

Heartbeats of Reflection

In quiet moments, thoughts arise,
Like echoes of a fading sigh.
The mirror holds a fleeting gaze,
Each heartbeat counts the passing days.

In shadows deep, secrets confide,
While memories in stillness bide.
I search for truths I'd thought I knew,
In pools of time, reflections brew.

Awake, I find a gentle peace,
As fleeting worries slowly cease.
With every pulse, a story told,
Of courage, dreams, and hearts of gold.

Through every tear and every laugh,
I trace the lines of my own path.
In heartbeats lost, in whispers found,
The essence of me is profound.

An ancient song, a tender tune,
The rhythm sways beneath the moon.
In the silence, I embrace,
The heartbeats of my own grace.

The Forgotten Symphony of Me

Among the notes of days gone past,
A melody, so sweet, yet vast.
It dances lightly on the breeze,
Whispers of joy, a soul's reprise.

Each chord a fragment of my days,
In harmony, lost in the haze.
The echoes linger, softly weep,
A symphony that stirs my sleep.

Faded rhythms seek the light,
As shadows twine with colors bright.
In every silence, music hums,
A calling forth from wretched drums.

The past, a stage, the future, a song,
In between, I've wandered long.
Yet through the haze, the notes still flow,
A tapestry of what I know.

So, I will sing, though faint the tune,
In every heart, a hidden rune.
The forgotten symphony of me,
Awaits to bloom, forever free.

Whispers Across the Chasm

In twilight's glow, the world seems wide,
Yet here we stand, with hearts as guides.
Across the chasm, voices call,
In whispered dreams that break the fall.

With every sigh that floats away,
A bond unseen in shadows play.
Though distance great, we still connect,
In silent words, a shared respect.

The nights are long, the stars they gleam,
While time unravels like a dream.
Each whisper carries hope anew,
In every curl, my heart finds you.

Through valleys deep, my spirit roams,
With every beat, it starts to foam.
These whispers bridge the gap of space,
In every moment, I embrace.

Though far apart, together still,
In quiet light, I feel the thrill.
Whispers across the chasm sway,
Connected souls, come what may.

Threads of Ancestors' Dreams

In every thread, a story spun,
Of battles fought, and victories won.
The tales of old, they weave and wind,
A tapestry of heart and mind.

From whispered hopes in twilight's fold,
The dreams of ancients, brave and bold.
Each choice they made, a path they carved,
In every life, their spirits starved.

I trace the lines with gentle care,
As echoes linger in the air.
In every stitch, their wisdom lies,
A guiding force, a sweet reprise.

Inheritances that intertwine,
Their dreams alive, within me shine.
Like roots of strength, they ground my soul,
In threads of love, we become whole.

Each heartbeat sings a timeless hymn,
An thread of light, on hope's own whim.
I honor those who came before,
In threads of dreams, forevermore.

Layers of the Unseen

Beneath the surface, shadows dance,
Whispers of secrets in every glance.
Veils of silence, gently unfold,
Stories untold, waiting to be bold.

In the quiet depths, echoes reside,
Memories cherished, nowhere to hide.
Colors merge where visions blur,
A tapestry woven, life's silent stir.

Each heartbeat carries tales of the past,
Moments fleeting, yet meant to last.
We search for meaning, in layers we find,
The essence of living, stitched in the mind.

Time weaves threads, some frayed, some tight,
In this vast darkness, we seek the light.
Through hidden realms, we learn to see,
The beauty within, in what may not be.

Every connection, a thread in the air,
Invisible bonds, a love we share.
In this grand tapestry, woven with care,
We find our truth, in layers laid bare.

The Soundtrack of Solitude

In the stillness, echoes arise,
The whispers of thoughts, beneath the skies.
Every heartbeat plays a soft refrain,
A melody drifting, sweet yet plain.

Moonlight bathes the silent night,
Stars become notes, shimmering bright.
Each sigh of the wind, a gentle song,
Navigating solitude, where we belong.

Rustling leaves join the symphony,
Nature's chorus, wild and free.
Footsteps crunching on the dampened ground,
In solitude's arms, peace is found.

Thoughts like shadows, dance in the dark,
Illuminated softly, each tiny spark.
With every breath, the silence grows,
An oasis of calm, where the spirit flows.

Transient moments, captured in sound,
In solitude's embrace, our solace is found.
The soundtrack lingers, whispers so true,
Amidst the silence, we start anew.

Undercurrents of Belonging

In the currents deep, we seek our way,
Tides of connection, come what may.
Ripples extend, beyond sight's gaze,
In unseen waters, we weave our phase.

Branches intertwine, where roots explore,
In shared dreams, we find the core.
Voices blend in a harmonious blend,
In the heart's realm, we learn to mend.

Waves of laughter, tears that flow,
In every heartbeat, true love's glow.
Elephants roam where friendships grow,
In this tapestry, we're never alone.

The winds carry tales from far and wide,
Rich with laughter, joy, and pride.
Unified spirits, bound by grace,
In this ocean of life, we find our place.

As we navigate the endless sea,
Undercurrents guide you and me.
In each embrace, in every song,
We discover our truth, where we belong.

Portraits in the Wind

Gentle breezes capture the scene,
Every soft whisper, a dream unseen.
In the rustling leaves, stories unfold,
Portraits painted, vibrant and bold.

Fragments of laughter carried afar,
Flying like kites, beneath the stars.
Each gust a canvas, colors awash,
Life's fleeting moments, in every brush.

Time flutters past like a dappled hue,
Moments remembered, both old and new.
In the fluttering pages of dreams, we find,
Portraits of lives interwoven, entwined.

Through meadows and valleys, the wind tells it all,
Each sigh a reminder, we rise and we fall.
Creatures and whispers compose the refrain,
In nature's gallery, joy and pain.

The sky bears witness to hearts that roam,
Chasing the currents, we search for home.
In each gust of life, a tale to ascend,
Portraits captured, in the wind's gentle bend.

Fragments of the Heart

Scattered pieces on the floor,
Whispers of what came before.
Memories woven in time's seam,
A tapestry frayed, a distant dream.

Echoes linger in the air,
Silent cries of love and care.
Each shard holds a story untold,
In the silence, they unfold.

A gentle touch, a fleeting glance,
Lost in the shadows of chance.
Yet hope springs from each fragment's light,
Guiding the way through the night.

Time beckons, we must mend,
Letting go, yet we extend.
With every heartbeat we reclaim,
The essence of love still remains.

In the fragments, we are whole,
A patchwork quilt of the soul.
Together, we rise, transcend the pain,
In the chorus, a sweet refrain.

Resonance in Quietude

In stillness grows a gentle sound,
Whispers of peace all around.
Nature breathes, a sigh so deep,
In quietude, we find our keep.

Rustling leaves, a soothing tone,
Softly played on nature's bone.
With every pause, a heartbeat swells,
Echoes of life, where silence dwells.

The sun sinks low, the shadows blend,
Moments cherished 'round the bend.
In twilight's glow, we gather near,
Whispers of love, serene and clear.

We dance with dreams in the twilight's hold,
Stories waiting to be told.
In resonance, a calm embrace,
Finding joy in the quiet space.

Each breath a note in a timeless song,
Together where we all belong.
In these echoes, we hear our hearts,
As quietude's magic gently starts.

The Mirror's Lament

Reflecting back, a fractured face,
In the glass, a haunted space.
Eyes that hold a world of sorrow,
Fading light, no bright tomorrow.

Shadows dance, they come and go,
Haunting whispers, a silent woe.
With every glance, a truth laid bare,
The mirror speaks, but who will care?

Desires clash with bitter fate,
A longing heart that hesitates.
As time flows like a river wide,
In reflection, our dreams collide.

The ghost of joy, a fleeting spark,
In the depths of each lonely heart.
Searching for light in a dim-lit room,
Yearning for life amidst the gloom.

Yet in the cracks, a glimmer shines,
A whisper from old, forgotten times.
The mirror laments, but still we see,
The beauty that lingers, still sets us free.

Chasing My Own Footsteps

Through winding paths, I roam alone,
Tracing shadows, a wayfarer's drone.
Memories whisper in the breeze,
Footsteps echo beneath the trees.

Each step a story, each turn a chance,
In the dance of fate, life's fleeting glance.
I gather pieces of where I've been,
Chasing dreams woven in the skin.

The road unfolds like a mystery,
Each corner hides a history.
Familiar places, faces and scenes,
Together stitched in heart's old seams.

Yet as I wander and seek the light,
The past entwines with the day and night.
In chasing whispers of what's been lost,
I find myself; love's sacred cost.

The journey's long, yet I embrace,
The fleeting moments, time can't erase.
In chasing footsteps, I find my way,
A traveler in the dance of day.

The Landscape of Longing

Across the hills, a whisper calls,
Rivers bend to distant thralls.
Every shadow holds a dream,
In twilight's glow, we softly beam.

The valleys ache with silent sighs,
Underneath the starlit skies.
Hope like wildflowers will bloom,
In the heart, dispelling gloom.

Mountains rise with ancient grace,
Each peak a story, a hidden place.
The heart roams, but cannot stay,
In this landscape, night and day.

Paths unexplored, we long to find,
Memories weave through the mind.
In every step, a silent plea,
To find the fate that sets us free.

A compass spun by tender hands,
Guides us through these longing lands.
In every breath, a tale unfolds,
The landscape waits, the heart it holds.

Tides of the Inner World

Waves of thought crash on the shore,
Ebbing dreams we can't ignore.
The tide pulls back, revealing light,
In the depths, shadows ignite.

The ocean sings of what's unknown,
A melody, both soft and grown.
Drifting thoughts like boats adrift,
In this vastness, our spirits lift.

Currents change with every breath,
Life's tides dance with love and death.
In the swirl, we find our place,
In the rhythm, a gentle grace.

Shores of silence, whispers swell,
Secrets hidden, none can tell.
Through the storm and calm alike,
We navigate the paths we hike.

Subtle waves, our feelings churn,
In this tide, we strive and learn.
From each wave, a lesson flows,
In the depths, our spirit grows.

Mosaic of Past Reflections

Fragments of time, a glassy sheen,
Moments captured, ever keen.
Colors blend in fading light,
We piece together wrong and right.

Each shard a story, sharp and clear,
Whispers echo, faint but near.
Through the cracks, we glimpse the glow,
Of a past that shaped our flow.

Lost in patterns, woven tight,
Memories dance in day and night.
In this mosaic, we find our way,
Guided gently by yesterday.

Fractured dreams, we hold them dear,
In their splendor, joy and fear.
With every piece, a path appears,
In the beauty, we shed our tears.

Reflections glimmer, soft and bright,
In the chaos, we find our light.
Mosaic heart, forever whole,
In each fragment, we share our soul.

Spheres of Silent Dialogue

In the stillness, we converse,
Words unspoken, souls immerse.
Eyes that meet, a language rare,
In this silence, we share our care.

Around us, echoes softly play,
Whispers linger, come what may.
In each moment, a thought takes flight,
Spheres of wisdom, pure delight.

Glimmers of understanding gleam,
In the quiet, we dare to dream.
Thoughts collide like stars in space,
In this dialogue, we find our grace.

Branches sway in the gentle breeze,
Nature listens, hearts at ease.
Through the air, a bond transcends,
These spheres of silence, true amends.

Hand in hand, we drift away,
In this unity, we sway.
It speaks the truths we cannot say,
In silent spheres, we find our way.

Chasing the Inner Muse

In quiet corners, shadows play,
Whispers dance, drift away.
Colors blend in twilight's hue,
Inspiration calls, breaking through.

A fleeting thought, a gentle spark,
Illuminates the waiting dark.
With open heart, I chase the light,
Crafting dreams with pure delight.

Moments linger, seize the day,
In every breath, I find my way.
The inner muse, a guiding force,
Leads me onward, my true course.

With pen in hand, I sculpt my fate,
Words untangle, liberate.
Each line a step, a journey new,
Chasing visions, pure and true.

In silence, magic starts to rise,
A symphony of unseen skies.
Guided by the stars above,
I find my muse, my heart's true love.

Silent Dialogues of the Mind

Within the stillness, thoughts collide,
A quiet storm, none can abide.
Whispers echo in the hollow,
The paths of dreams, I choose to follow.

In the chambers of my soul,
Fragments gather, seeking whole.
Voices speak in tender tones,
A chorus of my heart's own drones.

Between the lines, a story weaves,
Hidden truths in what deceives.
Each silence holds a word unspoken,
In the stillness, I am broken.

Through shadows cast, I seek the light,
Embracing both the dark and bright.
A canvas waits for thoughts to paint,
Silent dialogues, a sacred chant.

With every breath, I touch the void,
Where doubts are seen, and fears destroyed.
In the quiet, I find my peace,
The silent mind, a sweet release.

Layers of My Being

Beneath the surface, layers lie,
Echoes of dreams that make me cry.
In depths of night, I search within,
The stories told, where love has been.

Each layer peels, revealing pain,
In quiet tears, I find the gain.
Wounds that heal, like whispered song,
In every scar, I find I belong.

Fragile moments, woven tight,
A tapestry of loss and light.
I gather strength from every thread,
From shadows cast, new paths are bred.

Reflections deep, the mirror's gaze,
A dance of colors, an endless maze.
With every turn, I learn to see,
The layered depths that make me free.

In this journey, I embrace,
All the facets of my grace.
For in each layer, truth reveals,
The strength of heart, the power it wields.

The Soundtrack of Solitude

In the stillness, music plays,
A silent tune that softly sways.
Notes of peace, wrapped in the air,
A calming balm for whispered care.

Each heartbeat marks a subtle sound,
In solitude, my soul is found.
Melodies swirl in quiet dreams,
Where hope and solace find their themes.

The rustle of the leaves outside,
A symphony, where sorrows bide.
In every pause, a story hums,
The heart of night, where stillness comes.

Glimmers of light through shadowed trees,
Softly play, on the evening breeze.
Harmony dances, pure and free,
In the echoes of my reverie.

As dawn breaks gently, sound unfolds,
A tapestry of warmth extols.
With each new day, the music starts,
My solitude, a song of hearts.

Harmonies of the Forgotten

In whispers soft, the echoes play,
A tune from dusk, to dawn's new ray.
Lost melodies in silence fade,
Yet in our hearts, they gently shade.

A rhythm caught in twilight's grip,
Each note a dream, a fleeting trip.
Forgotten songs of years gone by,
Reviving hope as stars align.

The breeze hums low through endless trees,
Carrying tales on gentle seas.
In hidden nooks, the past takes flight,
Reviving joy in the quiet night.

A symphony of what once was,
Giving life to each silent pause.
Resounding deep within the soul,
A harmony that makes us whole.

So listen close, and you may hear,
The whispered tunes that draw us near.
In every heart, a song remains,
A harmony that breaks the chains.

Silhouettes of Forgotten Dreams

In twilight's glow, the shadows dance,
Silhouettes of dreams, a fleeting chance.
Whispers of hope in the fading light,
Echoes of wishes that took their flight.

Beneath the stars, memories gleam,
Fragile reflections of a lost dream.
Each shape tells stories of what could be,
A tapestry woven, wild and free.

Fleeting glimpses of the life once sought,
Each shadowed figure, a lesson taught.
In the dark, their outlines blend,
A fusion of beginnings and the end.

Yet hope prevails, like the morning sun,
Reframing dreams, making them one.
From shadows deep, new visions break,
A chance to rise, a chance to wake.

In every line, a path unfolds,
Silhouettes of dreams in tales retold.
With courage born from the night's embrace,
We step anew into the vast space.

The Language of Shadows

In the stillness, shadows creep,
Veiling secrets that secrets keep.
They speak in silence, soft and low,
In whispered tones, their stories flow.

There's poetry in their dark embrace,
A dance of light, a hidden trace.
Figures shift in the dim-lit night,
Translating truths from wrong to right.

Each flicker, a word unspoken,
Fate woven with threads unbroken.
In every flicker, a tale unfolds,
A language of life in whispers told.

As day surrenders to the moon's glow,
Shadows gather, and memories grow.
Through veils of darkness, wisdom shines,
In the language of shadows, all aligns.

Listen closely; they have much to say,
Guiding us through the night to day.
For in their silence, we find our way,
The language of shadows paves our way.

Cycles of My Truth

In every breath, a cycle spins,
A dance of life that never ends.
Through ups and downs, the lessons flow,
Cycles of truth that help us grow.

From springtime blooms to autumn's chill,
Each season's pulse, a guiding will.
In quiet moments, I reflect,
The turning tides, I can't neglect.

Each heartbeat drums a rhythmic tune,
A promise whispered by the moon.
In every cycle, I find my way,
Truth unfolding with each new day.

Through valleys deep and mountains high,
I seek the stars that fill the sky.
In all the changes, who am I?
Cycles of truth, I'll learn to fly.

So here I stand, with arms wide spread,
Embracing all that lies ahead.
For every truth I hold so dear,
Is part of me; I'll persevere.

Fragments of My Own Journey

In quiet moments, I reflect,
Pieces scattered, like a puzzle.
Each shadow holds a story,
A whisper of my past travels.

Footsteps echo on the path,
Every twist, a lesson learned.
I gather shards of who I am,
Embracing how the heart has yearned.

Through valleys deep and mountains high,
I search for meaning, find my way.
Each fragment tells a tale anew,
Of trials faced and hopes displayed.

With every dawn, a fresh embrace,
A chance to cherish what I've made.
The journey bends, yet I hold fast,
To dreams that shimmer, never fade.

So here I stand, a canvas wide,
With colors drawn from joy and pain.
Each fragment makes a vibrant whole,
A journey written, my own gain.

The Palette of Personal Touch

With every stroke, I find my voice,
Colors blend in dance and swirl.
A canvas rich with life's embrace,
My heart unfolds, my dreams unfurl.

A dash of blue for skies above,
A hint of gold for sunlit days.
Each hue reflects a cherished love,
In this creation, my soul stays.

Brush of sorrow, touch of grace,
Every layer tells a tale.
In shades of hope, I seek my place,
Through life's splashes, I will sail.

Textures rough and smooth connect,
In art, I find my pulse and beat.
The palette shines, a sacred space,
Where dreams and memories can meet.

In this creation, I am whole,
Each color sings a truth so clear.
The palette of my heart unfolds,
A masterpiece, I hold most dear.

Soft Cries, Loud Thoughts

In silence, whispers fill the air,
Voices clash within my mind.
Soft cries echo without a sound,
Loud thoughts wrap around, intertwined.

The smallest sigh holds weight untold,
A storm brews deep beneath my skin.
In solitude, battles unfold,
With every breath, I fight within.

Beneath the calm, a tempest lies,
Feelings dance in shadows fraught.
In the stillness, truth defies,
Light and dark weave through what's sought.

Shattered dreams often take their form,
In the chaos, I seek peace.
With soft cries, I mend the norm,
In loud thoughts, my heart finds release.

Thus, I walk this line of grace,
Where silence shapes the loudest thought.
In every layer, I embrace,
The beauty in the battles fought.

Dreamscapes of Unlived Lives

In twilight's grasp, I wander far,
Through dreamscapes woven lush and bright.
Each path reflects a distant star,
Stories whispered in the night.

Lives unlived beckon from afar,
A chorus sings of what could be.
I wander through each radiant scar,
In visions rich, I long to see.

Fleeting moments, colors blend,
A tapestry of dreams untold.
I grasp the threads, the shapes transcend,
And find in them a life of bold.

Each vision draws me close in kin,
A dance of hopes I can't reclaim.
Yet in this space, I feel the din,
Of dreams that echo, none the same.

So here I am, in dreams alive,
In every thought, a life takes flight.
These dreamscapes urge my heart to strive,
For all the lives I've yet to write.

The Voice Beneath the Surface

In the quiet depths, it waits,
A murmur lost in time.
Echoes of forgotten fates,
Awake to reason's climb.

Whispers swirl in darkened waves,
Secrets that the shadows keep.
The heart of silence gently laves,
Where dreams and reckoning sleep.

Beneath the mire, hope still glows,
A spark that dares to reach.
With each tide, the truth will flow,
A lesson life can teach.

Surface calm belies the strife,
That churns beneath the skin.
Finding depth within the life,
We learn to breathe again.

So listen close, as time unfolds,
This voice that sings of grace.
In the darkness, courage molds,
And rises to embrace.

Fractured Whispers of Tomorrow

Shattered dreams in morning light,
Fragments dance upon the air.
Voices calling from the night,
Stories lost in whispered prayer.

Riddles spun in silver threads,
Weaving hope through shadowed fears.
Each step forward, softly treads,
On remnants of our yesteryears.

In the echo of the past,
Future blooms like flowers bold.
Every moment fleeting fast,
Leaves us longing to be whole.

Captured thoughts drift like the mist,
Unraveling in gentle grace.
In the silence, truths persist,
Unveiling each neglected place.

Tomorrow's light will guide the day,
Mending wounds that time creates.
Fractured whispers will not sway,
As destiny patiently waits.

The Lullaby of Lost Selves

Hushed within the velvet night,
Memories softly hum.
Dreams entwined in pale moonlight,
Echoes of who we become.

Faded faces in the glass,
Reflections drift away.
Once we played, now shadows pass,
In the twilight's soft decay.

Every heartbeat tells a tale,
Of laughter, love, and pain.
In the stillness, we exhale,
What was lost may be regained.

Cradled in desire's arms,
We search for pieces whole.
The lullaby of ancient charms,
Sings to our wandering soul.

Rest now, sweet remnants of yore,
In the silence, find your place.
Together, we shall explore,
The beauty of our grace.

Tides of Internal Landscapes

Waves of thought crash on the shore,
Where mind and heart collide.
Each tide reveals an ancient lore,
Of all we try to hide.

In the quiet, currents pull,
Exploring realms untamed.
Mysteries both dark and full,
In shadows, we are named.

Sands of time slip through our hands,
As dreams begin to wane.
Yet within these shifting strands,
We find the strength in pain.

Mornings break with whispered light,
Kissing the scars we wear.
With each heartbeat, we ignite,
A flame that leads us there.

Learn to swim in depths unknown,
Embrace the ebb and flow.
In these tides, we find our own,
As internal landscapes grow.

The Sound of Being Alone

In silence deep, I hear the heart,
Whispers echo, worlds apart.
Shadows dance upon the wall,
In solitude, I hear the call.

Footsteps fade, the night unfolds,
A story told in silence bold.
The clock ticks loud, a gentle hiss,
Each minute lost, a fleeting bliss.

Thoughts adrift on waves of time,
A melody, a haunting rhyme.
The sound of being lost and found,
In quietude, the truth is crowned.

Yet in this space, I find my breath,
A canvas stretched, to life or death.
In being alone, I learn to see,
The beauty in what's meant to be.

From shadows cast, new light will spark,
In solitude, I leave my mark.
Embracing stillness, heartbeats twine,
In the sound of being, I am divine.

Unraveling the Unsaid

Beneath the surface, truths reside,
Words unspoken, hearts collide.
In crowded rooms, the silence grows,
A tapestry that no one knows.

Stitched in secrets, softly worn,
Silent battles, love reborn.
Eyes collide, sparks briefly flare,
Yet words remain, a vacant air.

Unraveling threads of what could be,
Bridges built, yet none can see.
The weight of thoughts, a fragile cage,
In quiet halls, we turn the page.

Fingers trace the lines of fate,
A dance of chance, Am I too late?
With every glance, the story grows,
Unraveling the unspoken throes.

In whispered winds, the tales emerge,
A symphony from silence purge.
For in the unsaid lies the key,
Unlocking what we long to be.

The Fabric of my Thoughts

Threads of memory, woven tight,
Colors blending in morning light.
Patterns formed by joy and pain,
A tapestry of loss and gain.

Each thought a stitch, each dream a seam,
In the loom of life, I find my theme.
Fleeting moments, held in place,
The fabric of my thoughts, a grace.

Worn and frayed, my edges show,
In the weft and warp, I ebb and flow.
Through laughter's thread, through sorrow's line,
The fabric whispers, "You're still fine."

In gentle hues, my truth unfolds,
A story rich with threads of gold.
Each memory a vibrant hue,
The fabric holds what's deep and true.

So I'll stitch on, through day and night,
With every thought, I weave my light.
A masterpiece of all I'm taught,
The fabric of my thoughts, my heart.

The Tapestry of Time

Woven strands of dusk and dawn,
In every moment, life is drawn.
The tapestry of days unspools,
Life's rich patterns, made with jewels.

Fleeting whispers of what has been,
Moments lost and moments seen.
The fabric shifts, the colors blend,
Threads of memories never end.

In laughter's echo, in sorrow's sigh,
The tapestry breathes, in truth, we fly.
The passage flows like a river wide,
Time's gentle hand, our constant guide.

Through seasons turning, hearts will meet,
In every challenge, stand, repeat.
A dance of years, a song divine,
In the tapestry of time, we shine.

With every breath, we leave a mark,
In threads of silver, in shades so stark.
Together we weave, together we climb,
In the wonder of life, the tapestry of time.

Traces of Unvoiced Thoughts

In shadows of the mind, whispers dwell,
Unsung melodies, stories to tell.
Fleeting moments like autumn leaves,
Caught in silence, the heart believes.

Fragments linger, soft and light,
Crimson dreams in the still of night.
Invisible threads pulling tight,
Echoes shimmer, fading from sight.

Thoughts unspoken, they roam free,
Silent hopes, lost in the sea.
Navigating through the unknown,
Finding solace in worlds not shown.

An echo lingers between the beats,
In a rhythm where longing meets.
Each glance a story, unconfessed,
In the heart's chamber, we are blessed.

A tapestry woven with care and grace,
In the quiet, we find our place.
Unseen currents that shape our way,
A journey held in the light of day.

The Pulse of Inner Worlds

In the depths where shadows play,
Thoughts pulse softly, night and day.
Fractal visions dance and twirl,
Echoing the heart's inner whirl.

Beneath the surface, tides do swell,
Secrets of the mind's deep well.
Resonance of fear, joy, and pain,
In this maze, we seek the gain.

Veils lifted by a gentle breeze,
Moments awaken with quiet ease.
The heartbeat of dreams softly hums,
A symphony where stillness comes.

Reflections shimmer on the stream,
Inside the core of every dream.
Terrains unseen, but felt so clear,
Consciousness whispers, drawing near.

Each thought a ripple, vast and deep,
In the silence, the mind will leap.
Harmony flows, and pulses rise,
In the depths, hidden worlds reside.

Harmonies of Hidden Truths

In the quiet, truths begin to sing,
Chords of wisdom that softly cling.
Whispers woven like threads of gold,
In the tapestry of stories told.

Layers of silence, waiting for light,
Illuminating shadows of night.
Unraveling the knots we weave,
In the solace, we learn to believe.

Frequencies dance in the air,
Unseen forces pulling us there.
Voices rising, a hidden refrain,
Melodies echoing joy and pain.

In the heart of the unexpressed,
Silent chords of life's great quest.
Every note a path to trace,
In harmonies, we find our grace.

The symphony swells, and we are drawn,
Into the light of a new dawn.
Together we weave what's yet to be,
In the chorus of possibility.

Reverberations of the Past

In whispers of time, memories flow,
Echoes of laughter, stories aglow.
The past, a canvas woven with care,
Each stroke a mark, a thought laid bare.

Shadows lingering, long and deep,
Within the folds, secrets we keep.
Patterns emerge from the echoes heard,
In the silence, our truths are stirred.

Moments linger like dew on grass,
Time's gentle hand, a delicate pass.
Tales of loss, hope intertwined,
In each heartbeat, the past aligned.

Fragments of joy, pieces of pain,
We dance through the storm and the rain.
Reverberations of steps once made,
In the rhythm of life, we are played.

A history that swells with grace,
In the mirror, we find our place.
The past, a guide, forever fast,
In the echoes, our shadows cast.

Reveries of an Untold Tale

In the hush of night, dreams unfold,
Whispers of stories long left untold.
Stars paint the sky with flickering light,
Guiding lost souls through the velvet night.

A river of memories flows like time,
Each moment a verse, in rhythm, in rhyme.
Chasing the echoes of laughter and tears,
Carving the path through the fabric of years.

Beneath the moon's gaze, secrets arise,
Unraveling truths in the silence of skies.
In shadows of time, every heart beats bold,
Reveries linger in stories retold.

Ghosts of the past dance in fading light,
Their soft sighs echo in the still of night.
With every heartbeat, a tale we weave,
In the tapestry of dreams, we believe.

So let the night cradle the tales yet spun,
In reveries whispered, the journey's begun.
With each fleeting thought, we find our way,
In the depths of our hearts, forever to stay.

Patterns in the Silence

In the quiet moments, whispers play,
Patterns of thought drift softly away.
In every shadow wrapped in the still,
Lies the gentle echo of time's quiet will.

Fingers of dusk glide softly through air,
Tracing the lines of secrets laid bare.
Beyond the noise, a world unfolds,
A story in silence, waiting to be told.

Each heartbeat resonates in the calm,
A soothing rhythm, a sacred psalm.
In the absence of sound, beauty is found,
Where the heart's quiet pulse is the only sound.

The stars above dance in velvet space,
Creating patterns, a cosmic embrace.
In the stillness, we learn to align,
With the patterns of peace that quietly shine.

Let us embrace the silence we seek,
In the moments of still, it's our souls that speak.
For in the quiet, the truth takes flight,
Revealing the patterns hidden from sight.

The Dance of Shadows Within

In the corners of mind, shadows twirl,
Whispers of thoughts in a delicate swirl.
Ghosts of the past weave tales of old,
In the dance of shadows, secrets unfold.

Flickers of light pierce the murky haze,
Illuminating paths through the foggy maze.
With every step, the present ignites,
Transforming the shadows into guided lights.

Echoes of laughter, whispers of woe,
The dance of shadows in ebb and in flow.
Every flicker tells a story anew,
Of the dreams we cherish, the ones we pursue.

Embrace the shadows, let them be your guide,
Through the depths of your heart, they will abide.
In the weave of your soul, let the dance begin,
For within the darkness, the light always wins.

So join in the waltz of the night, my friend,
With shadows of self, let our spirits blend.
In the dance of shadows, we learn to grow,
Embracing the depths of the self we know.

My Journey in Fractal Light

Through the prism of life, colors collide,
Fractal reflections of joy and of pride.
Each moment a pattern, intricate, bright,
Blossoming forth in the warmth of the light.

I wander through spaces where echoes abound,
In the realm of the lost, new treasures are found.
Textures of time weave a tapestry wide,
In the dance of creation, I find my stride.

Every turn shows a path newly drawn,
Like leaves that awaken with each break of dawn.
In spirals of thought, I discover the key,
Unlocking the wonders that dwell deep in me.

With every heartbeat, new patterns emerge,
A journey of fractals, a vivid surge.
In the glow of the now, my spirit takes flight,
Guided by hope in the fractal light.

So let me embrace the chaos and cheer,
For in every journey, there lies no fear.
In the language of light, I feel alive,
Through fractal dimensions, my spirit will thrive.

The Pulse of Remembering

In shadows deep, where whispers dwell,
The heart beats soft, a silent swell.
Each moment clings, a fleeting thread,
We trace the steps where once we tread.

The echoes call, a distant song,
In faded halls, where dreams belong.
Through time's embrace, we seek the light,
To find our way in the quiet night.

Faces blur in the softened haze,
Yet love survives in the ancient maze.
With every beat, the memories rise,
A tapestry woven, where truth lies.

The pulse of time, it beats anew,
In every laugh, in every rue.
We hold the past, a sacred space,
In every heart, a cherished place.

So let us dance, in twilight's gleam,
To the rhythm of a shared dream.
For in this pulse, we shall remain,
Forever bound, in joy and pain.

Patterns in the Echo Chamber

In corridors where echoes dwell,
The stories weave, a silent spell.
Patterns form in the whispered air,
Reverberate with secrets rare.

Voices blend, a choral swell,
Each tone a truth, a tale to tell.
In every nook, a silent shout,
Reminders of what life's about.

Fragments dance in the faded light,
Casting shadows of day and night.
In tangled thoughts, we seek to find,
The meaning held within the mind.

Patterns twist like branches high,
Reaching out to the endless sky.
In every heartbeat, echoes ring,
A melody of life we sing.

In chambers deep, reflections bloom,
Illuminating the darkest room.
For in these walls, our voices blend,
Creating patterns that never end.

Traces of the Unspoken

In silence thick, where shadows fall,
Lies a language beyond the call.
Traces left in the folds of night,
Whispers hinting at hidden light.

A glance, a sigh, a fleeting breath,
In quiet moments, we dance with death.
Secrets linger in the air,
Words unspoken, yet always there.

The weight of thoughts hangs in the breeze,
Like autumn leaves upon the trees.
We tread softly on unmarked ground,
Listening for the unheard sound.

Memories flutter like fragile wings,
Carrying the weight of untold things.
In the pauses, we connect the dots,
Finding solace in what time forgot.

So heed the signs in the stillness near,
For unspoken words can draw us near.
In every silence, there lies a thread,
Binding our hearts to what's unsaid.

The Lullaby of Memory

In twilight's glow, where dreams take flight,
A lullaby sings through the night.
Memories wrapped in a soft embrace,
Cradle the past in a sacred space.

Flickers of laughter, shadows of tears,
Echoes of joy that leave us in fears.
As twilight fades, the stars appear,
Their gentle whispers tug at the ear.

Each note a story, a tender call,
Resonates softly, the rise and fall.
The melody weaves through the fabric of time,
In every heartbeat, a gentle rhyme.

From childhood dreams to the weight of years,
Chasing the light through laughter and tears.
With every breath, we find our way,
Through the lullaby that guides our stay.

As dawn approaches, the song remains,
A bittersweet tune that still contains.
For in our hearts, the lullaby sings,
Of all the beauty that memory brings.

Unheard Chords of Existence

In shadows deep, where whispers lie,
The unsung notes of life drift by.
Each breath a song, in silence played,
Where dreams take flight, unafraid.

A melody of stars, so bright,
Hums softly in the quiet night.
Beneath the veil of time and space,
Resides a truth we all must chase.

In every heartbeat, rhythms flow,
A symphony that few can know.
Yet still we dance, though chords are lost,
Unraveling paths, no matter the cost.

With every tear, a note is spun,
A tale of battles lost and won.
In the echoes, we seek to find,
The unheard chords that shape the mind.

So hear the sounds beyond the gaze,
The flavours of a thousand days.
For in the quiet, life can sing,
An opus born from everything.

Mirrors in the Forest

In dappled light, the trees embrace,
With leaves that flutter, soft as lace.
Reflections dance upon the ground,
In this stillness, secrets found.

Each step among the ancient roots,
Calls whispers forth from gathered fruits.
Mirrors gleam where shadows play,
Revealing truths that guide the way.

Through canopies, the sunlight streams,
Illuminating hidden dreams.
Each branch a path to somewhere new,
Where nature's heart beats loud and true.

Echoes linger, soft and sweet,
In this magical, sacred retreat.
For every mirror shows and hides,
The forest's voice where beauty bides.

So listen close, let silence reign,
Among the whispers, joy, and pain.
In every glance, a world unfolds,
In forest's mirrors, life retolds.

The Hidden Gallery of My Mind

In corridors where shadows play,
Artistry begins to sway.
Canvas stained with every sigh,
In hues of laughter, love, and lie.

Brushstrokes wet with memories pale,
Each moment captured, vivid tale.
Frames unbroken, whispers loud,
A gallery where dreams are proud.

Fascinating glimpses caught in time,
Intricate views, a rhythmic rhyme.
Every piece a story told,
In colors rich, in patterns bold.

The light cascades through every door,
Illuminating wishes, hopes, and more.
Each thought a stroke upon the wall,
Creating beauty from the fall.

In this sanctuary, silence reigns,
Yet art explodes with vibrant veins.
The hidden gallery binds my heart,
In shadows, light, a world impart.

Paths Through Inner Wilderness

In tangled brambles, secrets grow,
Paths that wind where few dare go.
With every step, the wild reveals,
The echo of what truly feels.

Soft whispers drift on breezes mild,
Each twist a story, raw and wild.
Nature calls with a gentle hand,
To embrace the unknown, to understand.

Streams of thought like rivers flow,
Through valleys green where wildflowers blow.
Footsteps mark where moments meet,
In silence found, in heartbeats sweet.

Among the shadows, light will gleam,
In inner wilds, we chase a dream.
Through tangled paths, we discover grace,
In the wilderness of our own space.

So wander deep, let instincts guide,
Embrace the journey, cast aside.
For in the wild, both vast and grand,
We find our truth, and learn to stand.

The Hidden Narrative Within

Within our hearts, stories reside,
Whispers of dreams, secrets to confide.
Unfolding chapters, quiet and slow,
Every scar tells tales we hardly know.

In shadows deep, the truth is veiled,
A tapestry woven where hope has sailed.
Hidden in silence, our thoughts intertwine,
Each thread a testament, strong and divine.

Echoes of laughter, sorrows untold,
Moments of warmth in the bitter cold.
A confluence of paths, where we've been,
The hidden narrative lives within.

Time unfurls pages, memories weave,
In the quiet corners, we learn to believe.
Whispers of life in the still of the night,
A cherished reflection, a soft golden light.

Every heartbeat, a story begins,
Past and present, where life truly spins.
Eternal and rich, like stars that have shone,
The hidden narrative, ours to own.

Puzzles of Unanswered Questions

In the depth of night, shadows take flight,
Questions abound, obscured from the light.
What lies beyond the horizon we chase?
In whispers of doubt, we search for grace.

Fragments of truth glimmer and fade,
Mysteries linger, decisions delayed.
Paths intertwine, yet clarity's lost,
Every answer demands a new cost.

Sifting through chaos, we yearn to discern,
The riddles of life, for knowledge we yearn.
Where does love lead when hearts start to sway?
In puzzles of time, we drift and delay.

Questions ripple deep, like stones in a stream,
Each thought a reflection, a fleeting dream.
Unraveled in moments, like threads coming loose,
Puzzles unending, with no clear excuse.

In silence we gather and ponder the vast,
The weight of the past, a shadow it casts.
Yet hope is a beacon that shimmers in night,
Through puzzles of life, we strive for the light.

The Still Voice Beneath the Noise

Amidst the clamor, a whisper is heard,
A gentle reminder, soft yet unheard.
It speaks through the chaos, a calming embrace,
A still voice of wisdom, we long to trace.

In moments of tempest, when tempers ignite,
That quiet reassurance brings peace to the fight.
It dwells in our hearts, a sanctuary true,
Guiding us onward, in all that we do.

Turbulent currents can drown out the sound,
Yet beneath the surface, calmness is found.
In deep contemplation, we find our own way,
That still voice within guides us day after day.

When doubts cast shadows and fears come alive,
Listen for echoes that help us survive.
In stillness, we gather the strength to choose,
The quietest whispers are never to lose.

Each breath we take holds a promise unseen,
A thread of connection in all that has been.
Through noise and distraction, it reaches our core,
The still voice beneath, forever we'll adore.

Canvas of Lasting Impressions

On the canvas of time, we paint our dreams,
Colors of laughter, in shimmering streams.
Brushstrokes of kindness, vivid and bright,
Each moment captured, a flicker of light.

With every encounter, a mark left behind,
Impressions of love, forever entwined.
Handprints of memories, etched in the air,
A testament to connections we share.

Through trials and triumphs, we find our art,
Sculpting our stories, each beat of the heart.
Textures of pain, yet joy intertwined,
The canvas of life, where we seek and we find.

In strokes of compassion, we foster the hope,
Creating a masterpiece, learning to cope.
Life's beauty reflected in hues we embrace,
A canvas of impressions, love's warmest trace.

So let us create with passion and grace,
A tapestry woven, a shared sacred space.
When our time has ended, and shadows grow long,
The canvas we've painted will echo our song.

Rediscovering the Unforgotten

In shadows cast where memories dwell,
Whispers of time weave tales to tell.
With fragile hands, we touch the past,
Awakening dreams that everlast.

In twilight's glow, forgotten grace,
The heart can find its sacred space.
Echoes linger in the fading light,
Guiding souls through the endless night.

Amid the ruins, hope arises,
Rekindled flames and bright surprises.
A tapestry of lost and found,
In every silence, love unbound.

Through winding paths of faded lore,
We gather strength as we explore.
Each step we take, a gentle sigh,
Rediscovery before goodbye.

With every breath, we paint anew,
The canvas wide, with hues so true.
In every heartbeat, past's embrace,
A timeless dance, a sacred space.

Echoes in the Quiet Chamber

In silent rooms where shadows play,
Whispers of thoughts drift far away.
Dusty corners hold secrets tight,
Echoes whisper through day and night.

Beneath the stillness, stories breathe,
Moments linger, never to leave.
Pensive echoes, soft and clear,
Call us closer, draw us near.

Within the silence, hearts align,
A symphony of the divine.
Each lingering sound a cherished gift,
In quiet chambers, our spirits lift.

Time flows gently in this space,
Lending comfort, warm embrace.
Memories flutter, spirits rise,
In whispered tones, the world complies.

Through echoes sweet, we learn to see,
The beauty in simplicity.
With every breath and every sigh,
We find our truth, and never lie.

The Art of Solitary Exploration

In solitude, the heart takes flight,
A canvas blank, pure and bright.
Paths unfold in quiet grace,
Each step a journey to embrace.

With open eyes, the world in view,
Nature sings in shades of blue.
Winds of wisdom kiss the trees,
Whispers carried on the breeze.

Mountains stand, steadfast and true,
Inviting seekers, bold and few.
In valleys deep, where shadows creep,
Secrets lean, their promises keep.

Every moment holds the key,
To understanding, wild and free.
In isolation, thoughts expand,
Exploration leads to something grand.

In every heartbeat, art is born,
From roots of silence, dreams are torn.
The art of solitude's embrace,
Transforms each life, a sacred space.

Veils of the Inner Serenity

Behind the veil, so softly spun,
Lies the essence of everyone.
A tranquil heart, a quiet mind,
In stillness, freedom we shall find.

Layers deep, the soul does shine,
Wrapped in dreams, the pure divine.
In gentle whispers, truth reveals,
The strength in silence that soul heals.

Through waves of calm, the spirit flows,
In hidden realms where wisdom grows.
A dance of light, a sacred trust,
In quietude, we rise from dust.

With every breath, the world aligns,
In harmony where nature binds.
Veils unfold with grace anew,
Revealing depths we never knew.

In moments cherished, timeless grace,
The heart finds strength in its embrace.
Veils of serenity softly kiss,
A haven found in quiet bliss.

www.ingramcontent.com/pod-product-compliance
Ingram Content Group UK Ltd.
Pitfield, Milton Keynes, MK11 3LW, UK
UKHW032217171224
452513UK00010B/474